MACHINES BUILT AROUND YOU

Tailored Automation that Reduces Dependence, Waste, and Cost

AF518692

MACHINES BUILT AROUND YOU

Tailored Automation that Reduces Dependence, Waste, and Cost

Krishan Kumar

Available on amazonkindle

Worldwide Published by

Pendown Press
PREMIUM BUSINESS PUBLISHER

PENDOWN PRESS LLP

An ISO 9001 & ISO 14001 Certified Co.,

Regd. Office: 3767A, Kanhaiya Nagar,

Tri Nagar, Delhi-110035

Ph.: 8130886000, 9650072927, 8595249536

E-mail: info@pendownpress.com

Branch Office: 1A/2A, 20, Hari Sadan, Ansari Road,

Daryaganj, New Delhi-110002

Ph.: 011-45794768

Website: PendownPress.com

Edition: 2025

Price: ₹ 299

ISBN: 978-93-7217-031-3

All Rights Reserved

All the ideas and thoughts in this book are given by the author and he is responsible for the treatise, facts and dialogues used in this book. he is also responsible for the used pictures and the permission to use them in this book. Copyright of this book is reserved with the author. The publisher does not have any responsibility for the above-mentioned matters. No part of this publication may be reproduced, distributed, or transmitted in any form or by any means, including photocopying, recording, or other electronic or mechanical methods, without the prior written permission of the publisher and author.

Layout and Cover Designed by Pendown Graphics Team

Printed and Bound in India by Thomson Press India Ltd.

Dedication

This book is dedicated to my parents, Late Smt. Atro Devi & Late Sh. Mahender Singh Yadav, for their unconditional love, sacrifices, and the strength they gave me to rise every time life knocked me down. Their blessings lit the path even when there was no light.

TABLE OF CONTENTS

Bonus Chapter

PREFACE

Some journeys begin with a blueprint. Mine began with a broken machine and a desire to fix it—not just once, but better every time.

This book is very close to my heart. I did not write it to show off knowledge or impress anyone. I wrote it because I have spent years working with machines, people, problems, and solutions and I felt it was time to bring it all together in one place.

If you're someone who wants to build better machines… or run smoother operations… or just understand how things can be done in a smarter way, then this book is for you.

You don't need to be an engineer or a big business owner to read it. You only need curiosity and the desire to do something better. That's it.

This book might not be perfect. But every page has come from real experiences—what I've seen, learned, struggled with, and solved. That's why it's written in simple language, without complicated terms.

I believe learning is for everyone. Whether you're just starting your career or already running a factory, if this book helps you even 1%, then my effort is worth it.

I want to thank each reader for giving their time to this book. I'm not a professional writer—just someone who has built machines with love, and now words with the same.

With Warm Regards,

Krishan Kumar

ACKNOWLEDGEMENTS

A huge thank you to everyone who's been part of this incredible journey! Your love, support, and guidance have meant everything to me. I'm so grateful for all the discussions, helpful feedback, and expert advice that have made this book a reality.

Whatever I have achieved in life would have been impossible without the blessings and values instilled by my parents. Though they are not with me today, their love, sacrifices, and teachings continue to guide me every single day. The wings I have today were built by their faith in me.

To my incredible mentor, Sh. Akshar Yadav, thank you for sharing your wisdom and expertise with me. Your teachings have been invaluable, and I'm honored to have learned from you.

To my loving wife, Asha Yadav, and our two lovely kids, Aman and Bhuvika — thank you for being my biggest cheerleaders! Your love and encouragement have kept me going, even on the toughest days.

I thank my entire team for supporting the company during my toughest time in 2018, when I was almost bedridden for around 10 months.

A special acknowledgement goes to Dinesh Verma and his exceptional team at Pendown Press. From the initial concept to the final manuscript, their support and expertise have made this book possible.

And I want to extend my heartfelt thanks to everyone who's been part of my journey over the past 27 years. Your contributions, big or small, have been invaluable to me.

Without the support of all of you, it would not have been possible for me to move forward with confidence.

AUTHOR'S CORNER

"Partner in Your Growth Journey to Reduce Manufacturing Cost"

Hi, I'm Krishan Kumar, an expert in Industrial Automation and the founder of **Atma Autotech Engineers Pvt. Ltd.** I come from a small village called **Saidbher**, located on the Baghpat-Meerut Road.

My journey began in humble surroundings. My early education took place in my village, but due to my father's illness, I had to frequently shift between Delhi and my village, which disrupted my studies.

Despite the challenges, I completed my 12th standard while living in the village, earning by tutoring other students. I still remember those nights with no electricity, studying and teaching by lantern light.

Thinking Towards Automation

Even during my school days, I was fascinated by automation. I used to imagine a radio with buttons for pre-programmed station selection. Back then, station selection was done using a mechanical thread moved by a rotary knob.

After completing Class 12, there were no opportunities for higher education in my village, so I moved to Delhi in 1988. I first enrolled in B.Sc. at MMH College, Ghaziabad, and in 1989, I was selected for the Mechanical Engineering program at Government Polytechnic, Ghaziabad.

In September 1992, I completed my diploma and began my professional journey with Superfill Engineers, earning ₹1,000/ month. At Superfill, I learned about the manufacturing of Jigs & Fixtures.

After 1 year and 9 months, I joined Minda Industries as an Assistant Engineer in Production Engineering. There, I designed and developed **test rigs for automotive electric switches and locks**. I also set up a **calibration testing facility**. While working full-time, I pursued a Post Diploma in Tool Design from TRTC, Wazirpur.

In 1997, I was selected to visit Japan for an LCS test rig development project — an experience that greatly influenced my mindset around precision engineering.

Even during college, I was always curious and hands-on. I did the electrical wiring of my home and helped electronics students build their projects during my diploma.

Visiting Japan helped me develop a strong work ethic and gave me exposure to advanced industrial technologies. It fostered an engineering mindset rooted in **precision, innovation**, and **discipline**.

In July 1998, I decided to take a leap of faith and started my own business — **focusing on test rigs and industrial automation**. At that time, my salary was just ₹10000 /- per month, but I believed in my vision. I started with just two employees.

Today

- 130+ employees in Automation, and 425+ overall team strength
- 4000+ automation solutions delivered
- Serving 100+ clients

We've developed machines for the **automotive, switchgear, smart meter**, and **other industries**.

There's nothing I enjoy more than helping businesses achieve their goals. As a trusted supplier of **Special Purpose Machine (SPM) manufacturing**, I've worked across industries to provide **100% customized solutions** for **assembly & testing.**

For the past 27 years, my company, Atma Autotech , has been a leader in the SPM manufacturing space. We've helped many businesses—both big and small—transform their production processes and stand out from the competition.

We're proud of our track record of excellence and our unwavering commitment to innovation, quality, and customer satisfaction. I invite you to explore what Atma Autotech has to offer.

Today, We Operate Across Three Verticals:

1. Special Purpose Machine Manufacturer
2. Plastic Parts & Mold Manufacturing
   - 27+ injection moulding machines ranging from 60 to 850 tons
3. Wire Harness & Cable Manufacturing

INTRODUCTION
IMPORTANCE OF SPMS IN MODERN MANUFACTURING

"The machine doesn't fail in a day.
It whispers before it screams."

Special Purpose Machines (SPMs) play a **pivotal role** in transforming manufacturing systems into high-efficiency, high-productivity, and low-cost operations. As the demand for customized, precise, and fast production grows across industries, the limitations of general-purpose machines become more evident. This is where SPMs step in — **engineered to perform specific tasks with speed, accuracy, and consistency**.

1. **Productivity Enhancement**

   SPMs are designed for repetitive, high-volume tasks. Unlike general-purpose machines that require frequent setup changes, SPMs are tailored for a fixed operation, drastically **reducing cycle time** and **increasing throughput**. One SPM can often replace multiple conventional machines, enabling faster production with fewer operators.

2. **Consistency and Precision**

   In industries like automotive, aerospace, and electronics, even a minute deviation in dimensions can lead to failure. SPMs deliver **high precision and repeatability** due to custom jigs, fixtures, and automation, reducing human errors and ensuring **uniform product quality**.

3. **Cost Efficiency**

   Though the initial investment may be higher, SPMs significantly **reduce labor, rework, and downtime costs** over time. They also consume less energy per unit produced and often have longer lifespans due to optimized operations.

4. **Reduced Human Dependency**

   SPMs are ideal for operations that are **hazardous, monotonous, or require extreme accuracy**. By automating these tasks, SPMs reduce dependency on skilled labor and **enhance workplace safety**. This also helps mitigate the skilled labor shortage affecting many manufacturing sectors.

5. **Custom Solutions for Unique Problems**

   Off-the-shelf machines don't always meet the needs of specialized processes. SPMs allow manufacturers to **tailor machines specifically to their production needs**, whether it's for drilling, tapping, assembling, welding, or leak testing — achieving goals that standard machines can't match.

6. **Lean Manufacturing Support**

   SPMs support lean manufacturing principles by eliminating waste — of motion, time, and resources. With fewer setups, reduced scrap, and integrated quality checks, they align with continuous improvement and **Just-in-Time (JIT)** production systems.

7. **Faster Return on Investment (ROI)**

   With higher production rates and reduced operational costs, SPMs often provide a **quicker ROI** compared to standard machines, especially in high-volume environments. Their dedicated design and long-term durability make them a strategic investment for sustainable growth.

8. **Adaptability to Modern Technologies**

   Modern SPMs are fully compatible with **Industry 4.0** technologies such as:

- Digital twins for simulation and real-time optimization

- IoT sensors for predictive maintenance
- Cloud connectivity for remote monitoring and analytics
- Data integration with MES and ERP systems

This adaptability makes SPMs future-ready and scalable—ideal for smart factories aiming for efficiency, flexibility, and continuous improvement.

CHAPTER 1

Introduction to Special Purpose Machines

> *"Don't aim for perfection. Aim for progress you can repeat."*

What are SPMs?

SPMs stand for **Special Purpose Machines.**

These are machines specifically **designed and built to perform a specific task or a set of operations** that are either not achievable or inefficient with standard/general-purpose machines.

SPMs are customized for particular operations and are known for their **high speed, precision**, and **automation capabilities** in manufacturing environments.

Differences Between General-Purpose and Special-Purpose Machines

Here's a clear comparison of **General-Purpose Machines (GPMs)** vs. **Special-Purpose Machines (SPMs):**

GPM vs. SPM: Key Differences

Feature	General-Purpose Machines (GPM)	Special-Purpose Machines (SPM)
Purpose	Designed for a **variety of tasks**	Designed for a **specific task or operation**
Flexibility	High – can handle different jobs with tool changes	Low – limited to a particular function or set of operations
Productivity	Moderate	Very high for the specific task
Automation	Often manual or semi-automatic	Mostly fully automated
Operator Skill Requirement	Requires skilled operators for different setups	Minimal operator involvement once setup is complete
Setup Time	Longer – frequent changes in tools/ fixtures	Minimal – fixed setup for one job

Role in Enhancing Productivity, Accuracy, and Cost-Effectiveness

Special Purpose Machines (SPMs) play a crucial role in boosting **productivity**, improving **accuracy**, and achieving greater **cost-effectiveness** in modern manufacturing. Here's how:

1. **Productivity Enhancement**
   - **High-speed operation**: SPMs are engineered for specific, repetitive tasks and can operate much faster than manual or general-purpose machines.
   - **Minimal downtime**: Once set up, SPMs run continuously with very little idle time.
   - **Automation**: Integration with automation (robots, PLCs, sensors) reduces manual intervention and increases overall output.
   - **Parallel processing**: Many SPMs perform multiple operations (e.g., drilling, tapping, and checking) in a single cycle, significantly reducing cycle time.
   - *Example: A* ***camshaft drilling SPM*** *can complete operations in seconds that would take several minutes on a manual machine.*
2. **Accuracy & Consistency**
   - **Precision engineering**: SPMs are built with high-accuracy components, ensuring operations with micron-level tolerances.
   - **Repeatability**: They deliver consistent quality across thousands of units, with negligible deviation.
   - **Error reduction**: Human errors are minimized through **automation** and **fixed tooling**, ensuring stable and reliable output.

   Example: A leak testing SPM *provides consistent pressure readings and accurately detects defects with zero variation.*

Applications of Special Purpose Machines (SPMs) Across Industries

Special Purpose Machines (SPMs) are widely used across industries for their ability to perform dedicated tasks with precision, speed, and reliability. Here's a breakdown of their key applications:

1. **Automotive Industry**
   - **Applications**
     - Engine block drilling, boring, and honing
     - Gear and transmission assembly automation
     - Brake drum and disc machining
     - Axle shaft processing
   - **Benefits**
     - Increased production speed and consistency
     - Reduced human error in repetitive tasks
     - Custom fixtures for specific car models
2. **Electronics Industry**
   - **Applications**
     - PCB (Printed Circuit Board) drilling and component insertion
     - Soldering and inspection automation
     - Semiconductor packaging and testing
   - **Benefits**
     - High precision and miniaturization
     - Faster turnaround in high-volume manufacturing
     - Reduced damage to delicate components

3. **Medical Industry**
    - **Applications**
        - Surgical instrument machining (e.g., orthopedic implants)
        - Automated packaging of medicines
        - Catheter or stent assembly
    - **Benefits**
        - Sterile and consistent production environments
        - High-precision machining to meet strict medical standards
        - Customization for patient-specific devices
4. **Consumer Goods & Appliances**
    - **Applications**
        - Plastic injection molding automation
        - Assembly of small household items (e.g., fans, mixers)
        - Labeling and packaging
    - **Benefits**
        - Cost-effective mass production
        - Flexible tooling for product variations
        - Shorter lead times and faster market delivery
5. **Agricultural Equipment Manufacturing**
    - **Applications**
        - Machining of tractor parts
        - Hydraulic cylinder assembly
        - Soil tilling blade sharpening
    - **Benefits**
        - Rugged machines suited for heavy-duty processing
        - High throughput to meet seasonal demands
        - Reduced manual labor in large-scale manufacturing

6. Construction and Heavy Equipment

- **Applications**
  - Boring of large structural components
  - Bucket and chassis welding automation
  - Axle and joint machining
- **Benefits**
  - Efficient handling of heavy components
  - Improved precision in large-scale fabrication
  - Faster cycle times and enhanced durability

⚙⚙⚙⚙

CHAPTER 2

Classification of SPMs

> *"Every problem in automation is an invitation to think deeper."*

SPMs can be classified in various ways depending on their function, operation mode, or specific application. Understanding these classifications helps manufacturers choose the right machine for their unique production needs.

1. **Based on Function**

   SPMs are categorized according to the primary function they perform:

   - **Assembly SPMs**: Designed for automatic or semi-automatic assembly of components (e.g., switchgear assembly, appliance sub-assemblies).
   - **Machining SPMs**: Built for operations like drilling, milling, turning, grinding, etc.
   - **Testing SPMs**: Used for quality assurance processes such as leak testing, pressure testing, continuity checking, etc.
   - **Inspection SPMs**: Integrated with vision systems or sensors for dimension, surface, or alignment inspection.

2. **Based on Operation Mode**
    - **Manual SPMs**: Operated by hand, often used for basic or low-volume tasks.
    - **Semi-Automatic SPMs**: Combine manual loading/ unloading with automated processes like pressing, checking, or riveting.
    - **Fully Automatic SPMs**: Require minimal human intervention; incorporate PLCs, sensors, and robotics for end-to-end automation.
3. **Based on Application Type**

    SPMs are also named after the specific tasks or industries they serve:

    - **Drilling SPMs**
    - **Tapping SPMs**
    - **Leak Testing Machines**
    - **Riveting and Pressing SPMs**
    - **Soldering and Component Insertion SPMs**
    - **Balancing and Inspection SPMs**

    Each machine is engineered to deliver optimized performance for its particular role.

Case Examples

Real-world case studies demonstrate the measurable impact of SPMs in various industries:

Automotive Industry: Crankshaft Drilling SPM

➢ **Use Case:** A tier-1 supplier developed a multi-spindle SPM for crankshaft drilling.

- **Impact:** Reduced cycle time from **1.5 minutes to 30 seconds** per part.
- **Features:** Automatic loading/unloading, multi-station rotary table, in-process gauging.
- **Outcome:** Increased productivity by 200% with minimal operator intervention.

Electronics Industry: PCB Drilling SPM

- **Use Case:** BEL implemented CNC-based SPMs for high-speed drilling of PCBs.
- **Impact:** Achieved drilling accuracy within **±0.01 mm**.
- **Features:** Auto-tool change, vacuum bed holding, dust extraction system.
- **Outcome:** Enhanced reliability of defense-grade electronics while reducing manual errors.

Consumer Appliances: Washing Machine Drum Assembly SPM

- **Use Case:** An SPM was developed for riveting and balancing washing machine drums.
- **Impact:** Reduced assembly defect rate by **70%**.
- **Features:** Inline balancing system, servo-controlled riveting, smart error detection sensors.
- **Outcome:** Increased throughput with consistent build quality and reduced rework.

These examples show how SPMs make work faster, more accurate, and more cost-effective across industries.

CHAPTER 3

DESIGN FUNDAMENTALS

"A stable process beats a brilliant plan."

Machine Design Basics: Static & Dynamic Loads, Material Selection

Here's a **clear and concise overview of machine design basics**, focusing on **static & dynamic loads** and **material selection**—which are core concepts for anyone working with Special Purpose Machines (SPMs) or any type of mechanical system.

Machine Design Basics

1. **Static and Dynamic Loads**

   Static Loads

   - **Definition:** Loads that remain constant or change very slowly over time.
   - **Examples:**
     - Weight of machine parts
     - Fixture holding a component during machining

- **Design Consideration**
  - Focus on yield strength and factor of safety (FoS).
  - Simplified stress analysis using basic formulas (e.g., axial, bending, torsion).

Dynamic Loads

- **Definition:** Loads that vary with time due to motion, vibration, or impact.
- **Examples:**
  - Reciprocating parts like pistons or sliders
  - Gear meshing or rotating shafts
- **Design Consideration**
  - Consider fatigue strength, natural frequency, and vibration damping.
  - Use S-N curves (stress vs. number of cycles) for fatigue life analysis.
  - May require advanced tools like dynamic simulation or Finite Element Analysis (FEA).

2. **Material Selection**

Material choice directly affects performance, durability, weight, and cost.

Key Factors in Selection:

- **Mechanical Properties:** Strength, hardness, ductility, toughness
- **Thermal Properties:** Heat resistance, conductivity
- **Wear Resistance:** Especially for moving/sliding parts
- **Corrosion Resistance:** Important for medical, chemical, or outdoor use

- **Machinability & Weldability:** For ease of manufacturing
- **Cost & Availability:** Should be affordable and easily available to avoid delays and extra cost

Common Materials in SPM Design

Component	Common Materials	Reason
Machine frame/base	Cast iron, mild steel	Good damping, strength, cost-effective
Shafts & spindles	Alloy steel (EN24, EN19)	High strength & toughness
Guideways & slides	Hardened steel, nitrided steel	Wear resistance, smooth motion
Fixtures & tooling plates	Aluminum, tool steel	Lightweight (Al), hardness (tool steel)
Covers & panels	Stainless steel, polycarbonate	Aesthetic appeal, corrosion protection

Design Tip Summary

- **Always start with accurate load estimation**—overdesign wastes material; underdesign causes failure.
- In SPMs, focus on **stiffness, fatigue life**, and **vibration control**, especially at high speeds or precision levels.
- **Choose materials** not just for strength, but also for **ease of manufacturing** and **working conditions** (temperature, wear, corrosion).

Additional Design Considerations

- **Ergonomics and operator interface:** Ensure the machine is safe and easy to use
- **Component selection:** Bearings, motors, guideways, sensors, actuators
- **Compliance**: Follow relevant **design standards** and **safety norms**

CHAPTER 4

Control Systems and Automation

> *"The best designs are not the most complex—they're the most understood."*

Role of PLCs, HMIs, and SCADA in SPMs & Industrial Automation

Automation plays a crucial role in making Special Purpose Machines (SPMs) efficient, accurate, and intelligent. Let's look at how key control systems—**PLCs**, **HMIs**, and **SCADA**—work individually and together.

1. **PLC (Programmable Logic Controller)**

   Role:

   - Acts as the **brain of the machine**, executing logic-based operations.
   - Monitors sensors, controls actuators, and manages sequences automatically.

   In SPMs:

   - Controls machine cycles, clamping/unclamping, indexing tables, spindle operations.

- Ensures repeatability, accuracy, and interlocking for safety.
- Responds instantly to inputs like limit switches, proximity sensors, or emergency stops.

Example:

- A PLC manages the operation of a **multi-station drilling SPM**—once the part is loaded, it automatically sequences the drill heads, coolant flow, and part ejection.

2. **HMI (Human Machine Interface)**

Role:

- Provides a **user-friendly interface** between the machine and the operator.
- Displays real-time data, system status, alarms, and allows parameter settings.

In SPMs:

- Operators can start/stop cycles, select part programs, and view faults.
- Maintenance teams use HMIs to monitor I/O status and diagnostics.

Example:

- A touch-screen HMI lets the operators choose between **different part variants**, view live cycle times, and access troubleshooting guides.

3. **SCADA (Supervisory Control and Data Acquisition)**

Role:

- Provides **centralized monitoring and control** across multiple machines or processes.
- Collects and logs data, visualizes performance, generates reports, and issues alerts.

In SPMs / Plant-Wide Systems:

- Monitors multiple SPMs on a production line in real time.
- Tracks downtime, production counts, energy use, and machine health remotely.
- Supports preventive maintenance and data-driven decision-making.

Example:

- A SCADA dashboard shows the performance of 10 SPMs across shifts—highlighting one machine with frequent stops, and triggering a maintenance check.

How They Work Together

System	Primary Function	Level
PLC	Controls individual machine logic	Machine-level
HMI	Interface for operator input/output	Operator-level
SCADA	Supervises and monitors multiple systems	Supervisory-level

Benefits in Industrial Automation & SPMs

- **Faster troubleshooting**
- **Reduced human error**
- **Increased productivity**
- **Predictive maintenance via data**
- **Customizability for different product variants**

Pneumatics, Hydraulics, and Electro-mechanical Actuation

Here's a **detailed overview** of **Pneumatics, Hydraulics, and Electro-mechanical Actuation** — essential actuation methods used in **Special Purpose Machines (SPMs)** and industrial automation:

Actuation Technologies in Automation

1. **Pneumatic Actuation**

   How It Works:

   - Uses **compressed air** to move pistons or actuators.

   Key Features:

   - Fast response and simple control
   - Clean and safe (no leakage of harmful fluids)
   - Ideal for **light-duty** repetitive tasks

   Common Applications:

   - Clamping/unclamping parts
   - Actuating air cylinders for pushing/pulling
   - Blow-off or ejection of components

   Limitations:

   - Limited force (due to low pressure: 6–10 bar)
   - Less precise control
   - Noisy operation and energy loss due to compressed air leaks

2. **Hydraulic Actuation**

   How It Works:

- Uses **pressurized hydraulic fluid** (usually oil) to transfer power.

Key Features:

- High power density → delivers **very high force**
- Smooth motion under heavy load
- Suitable for **heavy-duty** industrial processes

Common Applications:

- Pressing, broaching, and shearing
- Lifting and lowering heavy components
- Forming operations in metal or plastic

Limitations:

- Risk of oil leaks (messy and maintenance-intensive)
- Requires regular maintenance (cooling & filtration)
- Slower than pneumatics for quick actions

3. **Electro-mechanical Actuation**

How It Works:

- Converts **electrical energy into mechanical motion** using motors (servo, stepper, etc.), combined with gears, screws, or belts.

Key Features:

- High **precision** and programmability
- Closed-loop control (position, speed, torque)
- Clean, quiet, and flexible

Common Applications:

- Robotic arms and linear actuators

- Multi-axis part positioning systems
- Automated tool changers
- Servo-driven slides or rotary tables

Limitations:

- Higher initial cost
- Sensitive to overloads and harsh environments
- Requires advanced control systems

Comparison Table

Feature	Pneumatics	Hydraulics	Electro-mechanical
Power Medium	Compressed Air	Hydraulic Oil	Electricity
Force Output	Low to Medium	High	Medium to High
Speed	Fast	Moderate	Variable, programmable
Control Precision	Low	Moderate	High
Maintenance	Low	High	Medium
Cleanliness	High	Low (oil leakage)	High
Best For	Simple, fast tasks	Heavy-load operations	Precise, flexible control

Selection Guidelines

Use Pneumatics if:	Fast, simple, low-cost motion is needed (e.g., ejectors, clamps).
Use Hydraulics if:	High force and rugged motion are required (e.g., presses, lifting).
Use Electro-mechanical if:	High precision, programmability, and automation are needed (e.g., CNC tables, vision-based sorting).

Integration with sensors and actuators

Integration of Sensors and Actuators in SPMs

1. **Role of Sensors in SPMs**

   What They Do:

   Sensors detect physical conditions and **provide real-time feedback** to the control system (PLC or controller). This feedback helps the machine make decisions and maintain safe, precise operation.

Common Types of Sensors

Sensor Type	Purpose	Example Use in SPM
Proximity sensors	Detect object presence/position	Confirm part loading before machining
Photoelectric sensors	Detect light interruption	Object detection on conveyor
Limit switches	Mechanical position sensing	Detect end-of-stroke for actuators

Pressure sensors	Monitor air/ hydraulic pressure	Ensure correct clamping pressure
Temperature sensors	Measure heat in tools/motors	Prevent overheating during extended operation
Encoders	Detect shaft/slide position	Used with servo motors for precise control
Vision sensors	Perform image-based inspections	Part presence, orientation, or surface defect checking

2. **Role of Actuators in SPMs**

   What They Do:

   Actuators **convert control signals into physical motion**. They are used for operations like clamping, pushing, rotating, and positioning.

Common Types of Actuators

Actuator Type	Motion Type	Example Application
Pneumatic cylinders	Linear	Part ejection, gate opening
Hydraulic cylinders	Linear	Pressing or forming operations
Solenoid valves	On/off fluid control	Control of air or fluid flow

Stepper motors	Precise rotational	Rotary indexing table
Servo motors	Closed-loop motion	Positioning slides, tool heads
Linear actuators	Linear/electric	Fine part positioning in assembly machines

3. **Integration Flow: How It All Connects**
    1. Sensors collect data → position, pressure, temperature, etc.
    2. Data is sent to PLC or controller (central logic unit)
    3. The PLC processes logic and sends signals to actuators
    4. Actuators perform motion or control functions (move parts, clamp, rotate, etc.)
    5. Feedback loops detect errors and make real-time corrections (e.g., if part is missing or pressure is too low)

Example: SPM for Automatic Drilling

➢ **Sensors**

- Proximity sensor checks if part is loaded.
- Limit switch confirms drill retract position.

➢ **PLC Logic**

- If both sensors give "OK", the drilling cycle starts.

➢ **Actuators**

- The pneumatic cylinder clamps the part.
- The servo motor feeds the drill spindle.
- Linear actuator retracts the drill after the operation.

Benefits of Sensor-Actuator Integration

- Increases automation & consistency
- Reduces manual errors
- Speeds up fault detection
- Enables intelligent, responsive machine behavior
- Supports Industry 4.0 (IoT ready, real-time monitoring)

Smart manufacturing & Industry 4.0 in SPMs

What Is Industry 4.0?

Industry 4.0 refers to the **4th Industrial Revolution**, where physical machines are connected with **digital technologies,** such as:

- IoT (Internet of Things)
- Big Data & Analytics
- Cloud Computing
- Artificial Intelligence (AI)
- Cyber-Physical Systems
- Smart Sensors and Actuators

What Is Smart Manufacturing?

Smart Manufacturing is the **intelligent use of data, automation, and connectivity** to improve production efficiency, flexibility, and decision-making.

How SPMs Fit into Industry 4.0

SPMs, traditionally built for rigid, repetitive tasks, are now evolving into **adaptive and data-driven systems**. Here's how they are becoming part of the Industry 4.0 ecosystem:

1. **IoT Integration (Industrial Internet of Things)**
   - SPMs are embedded with **sensors and connected devices.**
   - Data is collected in real time: temperature, vibration, spindle speed, tool wear, cycle time.
   - Enables **remote monitoring, predictive maintenance,** and **energy optimization.**

   Example: A connected SPM alerts the maintenance team when vibration exceeds threshold → Preventing downtime.
2. **Data Analytics & Predictive Maintenance**
   - Historical and live data are analyzed to detect **patterns and anomalies.**
   - Helps schedule maintenance **before breakdowns.**
   - Reduces unplanned stoppages and extends machine life.

   Example: A drilling SPM analyzes tool wear rate to predict when tool replacement is needed.
3. **Interconnected Systems (SCADA, MES, ERP)**
   - SPMs communicate with **SCADA, Manufacturing Execution Systems (MES),** and **ERP.**
   - Allows seamless coordination from **shop floor to top floor.**
   - Optimizes resource planning, inventory, and production flow.

   Example: An SPM auto-updates the MES with production count for real-time batch tracking.
4. **AI & Machine Learning in SPMs**
   - Used for **adaptive process control**, quality prediction, and **self-optimization.**
   - Machines learn from data to fine-tune their parameters over time.

Example: AI monitors output quality and adjusts feed speed to reduce rejection rate in real time.

5. **Digital Twin Technology**
   - A **virtual replica** of the SPM is created to simulate, monitor, and optimize the real machine.
   - Helps in fast prototyping, design testing, and remote troubleshooting.

   Example: A virtual model tests a new part variant cycle without stopping the real machine.

6. **Smart HMIs & Remote Access**
   - HMIs now provide dashboards, diagnostics, and cloud connectivity.
   - Engineers can monitor and update machine programs **remotely**.

   Example: A supervisor receives vibration alerts on mobile and checks machine status remotely.

Benefits of Smart SPMs in Industry 4.0

Benefit	Impact
Real-time monitoring	Faster response to issues
Predictive maintenance	Reduces unplanned downtime
Improved product quality	Through data-driven control and self-adjustment
Higher flexibility	Quick changeovers for different product variants

Energy efficiency	Through monitoring and optimization
Data-driven decision making	Better planning and traceability

From Rigid to Adaptive

Old SPMs = Rigid, single-task, isolated

Smart SPMs = Connected, flexible, responsive, and ready for the future

⚙⚙⚙⚙

CHAPTER 5

TOOLING AND FIXTURES

> *"Automation fails where assumptions win over analysis."*

Importance of Jigs and Fixtures in Precision Engineering

1. **What Are Jigs and Fixtures?**
   - **Jig**: A work-holding device that **guides the cutting tool** (e.g., drill jigs).
   - **Fixture**: A device that **securely holds and locates** the workpiece but **does not guide** the tool.

   Key difference: Jigs guide the tool; fixtures only hold the part.

2. **Role in Special Purpose Machines (SPMs)**

   SPMs are built for high-speed, repetitive tasks—where **accuracy and repeatability** are crucial.

   Jigs and fixtures ensure that parts are always positioned correctly, leading to uniform machining results cycle after cycle.

3. How They Improve Precision

Precision Factor	How Jigs/Fixtures Help
Repeatability	Maintain exact workpiece location across multiple cycles
Reduced Human Error	Eliminate reliance on manual measurement or alignment
Tool Guidance (in Jigs)	Ensures exact hole position, angle, and depth every time
Minimized Part Movement	Firm clamping prevents vibration, slippage, or misalignment
Consistent Reference Points	Use of uniform datum points ensure identical machining for all parts
Faster Setup Times	Standardized holding reduces setup time and operator dependency

4. Examples in Real-World Applications

- **Drilling SPM with Jig**
  - Jig holds the component and guides the drill bush.
  - **Result:** Holes drilled with identical spacing and angle every time.
- **Milling Fixture in an SPM**
  - Fixture locks part into position with dowel pins and clamps.
  - **Result:** Identical cuts, reduced tolerance variation.
- **Welding Fixture**
  - Holds multiple parts at exact angles and distances.
  - **Result:** Perfectly repeatable weld joints in robotic welding setups.

5. Benefits in Precision Manufacturing

Benefit	Impact
Higher product quality	Better dimensional accuracy, fewer defects
Faster production	Reduced setup and checking time
Lower rejection rate	Consistent part accuracy and surface finish
Better tool life	Stable clamping reduces tool wear
Increased machine efficiency	Supports high-speed, unattended machining

In Summary

Jigs and fixtures are **fundamental tools** in any precision manufacturing setup. In SPMs, where the goal is **repeatability at scale**, they ensure:

- **Consistent part alignment**
- **Accurate machining**
- **Stable and reliable operation**

They **bridge the gap between machine capability and real-world performance**, making precision possible in mass production.

Design Principles for Custom Tooling

Custom tooling refers to specially designed **tools, jigs, fixtures, or inserts** tailored for a particular job, part geometry, or machine. Precision tooling is essential for quality, efficiency, and repeatability in modern manufacturing.

1. **Define the Objective Clearly**

   Start by identifying:

   - The part to be machined
   - The operation to be performed (e.g., drilling, turning, clamping)
   - The machine on which it will be used
   - Production volume (low, batch, mass)

   Why it matters: A robotic welding jig is very different from a fixture for a CNC mill.

2. **Precision & Repeatability**

   - Ensure **tight tolerances** where required.
   - Incorporate **locating pins, dowels, or reference surfaces**.
   - Provide **repeatable clamping** without distorting the part.

   Tip: Always design to maintain **geometric consistency** across multiple workpieces.

3. **Rigidity & Strength**

   - Tooling must withstand operational forces **without flexing or vibrating**.
   - Use **robust materials** (e.g., EN8, hardened tool steel, aluminum alloys).
   - For cutting tools, ensure **short overhangs** and rigid holders to avoid chatter.

   Tip: Design for **stiffness first**, then optimize for weight or cost.

4. **Quick Setup & Changeover**
   - Design for **minimum tool change time.**
   - Include features like:
     - Quick-release clamps
     - Modular elements (base + interchangeable inserts)
     - Tool-free locking mechanisms

   Smart idea: Use dowel and bolt combinations to ensure fast and accurate re-installation.

5. **Accessibility & Ergonomics**
   - Tooling should be **easy to load, unload, and inspect.**
   - Avoid sharp edges, deep pockets, or unsafe clamps.
   - Ensure **good visibility** and **sufficient clearance** for tools or probes.

   Tip: Test tooling on a mock setup or CAD simulation before fabrication.

6. **Alignment & Location Accuracy**
   - Use **3-2-1 locating principles** to constrain part movement.
   - Prevent misalignment due to part variations.
   - Maintain consistent **datums and reference faces.**

   Why it's important: Mislocated parts lead to dimension failures or rework.

7. **Material & Surface Finish Selection**
   - **Tool Steel / EN-series** for wear-prone areas
   - **Aluminum** for lightweight tooling
   - Hardened bushes in jigs for **drill guidance**
   - Surface coatings (e.g., black oxide, chrome, anodizing) for durability

8. **Inspection & Validation Features**
   - Include **gauge points or reference slots** to allow in-process inspection.
   - Design tools that allow for **easy part checking without removal**.

   Pro tip: Include wear indicators or visual guides for maintenance triggers.

9. **Maintainability & Modularity**
   - Design tooling in **modules**: base, clamps, inserts, guides.
   - Replace **wear parts** (like bushes, pins, jaws) easily.
   - Keep **standard fasteners** and minimal unique components.

10. **Cost vs. Performance Trade-Off**

    Balance:
    - Precision requirements
    - Production volume
    - Material and machining cost
    - Tool life and reusability

    Tip: For high-volume jobs, invest in **hardened, durable tooling**; for prototypes or short runs, consider **3D printed or modular setups**.

Summary: Design Checklist

Aspect	Checklist
Functionality	Meets operational requirements
Accuracy	Locates and holds parts precisely
Rigidity	Withstands cutting/operational forces
Ergonomics	Safe and easy to use

Modularity	Supports quick changeovers and replacement
Maintainability	Easy to service and inspect
Material Suitability	Durable and fit for purpose
Cost Efficiency	Justified for the production volume

Quick-Change Tooling Systems

What Is Quick-Change Tooling?

Quick-change tooling systems are **mechanical setups that allow tools, dies, or fixtures to be swapped rapidly—without the need for re-alignment, re-measurement, or manual tool-setting**.

They significantly reduce machine downtime, making production **faster, leaner, and more flexible**

Why It's Important

In SPMs and mass production environments, even small delays in tool changeovers can lead to:

- Reduced output
- Increased labor costs
- Higher chances of setup errors

Quick-change systems help achieve:

- **Faster changeovers**
- **Higher uptime**
- **More product variety with the same machine**

Common Types of Quick-Change Tooling Systems

System	Description	Use Case
Quick-change tool holders	Tooling mounted on modular holders that can be released/locked with a single action	CNC machining, drilling heads
Zero-point clamping systems	Pneumatic or mechanical clamping systems with precise locating pins or balls	Fixture mounting on machining tables
Magnetic quick-change plates	Use magnetic force to hold and quickly release molds or dies	Injection molding or press tools
Cam lock and wedge systems	Use mechanical levers or cams to release and clamp dies or inserts	Stamping or forming dies
Automatic tool changers (ATC)	Used in CNC machines or robotic SPMs to change tools without human intervention	Multi-tool operations with minimal downtime

Features of Effective Quick-Change Systems

- **Repeatable positioning** (within microns)
- **Change time < 1 minute**
- **Self-centering or self-locking** mechanisms
- **No need for re-zeroing or manual tool setting**
- **Secure and rigid clamping** under operational loads

Benefits in SPMs & Lean Manufacturing

Benefit	Impact
Reduced downtime	More productive machine hours per shift
Less operator skill needed	Faster training, safer and easier handling
High flexibility	Easy to switch between part types or variants
Maintained precision	Eliminates realignment or offset errors
Cost savings	Lower setup costs, higher overall equipment efficiency (OEE)

Example in Practice

Scenario: An SPM performs 3 operations: drilling, chamfering, and tapping.

With a quick-change spindle tool holder:

- All 3 tools are pre-mounted and pre-aligned.
- The operator switches between tools in **under 30 seconds**.
- No re-zeroing or offset adjustment needed.

Best Practices for Implementation

- Use **modular design** in all fixtures and holders.
- Standardize tool interfaces across different machines.
- Keep spare tool sets ready to avoid production delays.

Pair with **digital tool libraries** for smart tool tracking.

CHAPTER 6

MANUFACTURING AND ASSEMBLY

> *"Ignoring small issues is the fastest way to grow a big one."*

Sourcing & Fabrication of Machine Components

1. **Types of Machine Components**

   SPMs consist of a mix of **standard** and **custom components**:

Component Type	Examples
Standard Parts	Bearings, fasteners, guides, couplings, bushings, linear rails
Custom Fabricated	Machine base frames, special brackets, housings, enclosures
Machined Parts	Shafts, cams, gears, spindles, jigs, tool holders
Bought-Out Items	Motors, cylinders, PLCs, sensors, HMIs, valves

2. Sourcing Strategy

A. Standard Components:

- Source from certified industrial suppliers (e.g., SKF for bearings, Festo for pneumatics).
- Use catalogue parts to reduce lead time and ensure consistent quality.

B. Bought-Out Items:

- Choose based on:
  - Performance specs (torque, speed, voltage, etc.)
  - Interoperability with PLCs and HMIs
  - Warranty and support availability
- Always verify **brand reliability** and **regional availability**.

C. Custom Fabricated Parts:

- Sourced from local or specialized **fabrication shops**.
- **Ensure:**
  - Dimensional accuracy (GD&T)
  - Required surface finish
  - Material test certificates (if needed)

3. Fabrication Processes

Process	Used For	Common Methods
Machining	Shafts, housings, precision tools	Turning, milling, boring, grinding, EDM
Fabrication/ Welding	Base frames, brackets, guards	MIG/TIG welding, flame cutting, plasma cutting
Sheet Metal	Panels, covers, operator consoles	Laser cutting, bending, powder coating

Surface Treatments	Corrosion or wear resistance	Anodizing, hard chrome, nitriding, painting

4. **Design for Manufacturability (DFM)**

   Design parts to:

   - Use **standard sizes** and material profiles
   - Minimize tight tolerances unless absolutely required
   - Allow **easy fixturing and machining**
   - Avoid complex geometries unless required

   Tip: Involve fabricators early in the design stage to reduce rework and cost.

5. **Quality Control in Sourcing**

   - Perform **Incoming Quality Inspection (IQC)** for all fabricated or bought-out items.
   - Check:
     - Material grade
     - Dimensional accuracy (with calipers, CMM, gauges)
     - Finish (as per drawing)
     - Functional tests (e.g., motor RPM, cylinder stroke)

   Best Practice: Use standardized inspection checklists and maintain records for each component.

6. **Supply Chain Considerations**

Factor	Why It Matters
Lead time	Affects project deadlines and delivery schedule
Supplier reliability	Impacts quality and consistency

Cost vs. quality balance	Must match budget without sacrificing function
Localization	Reduces logistics delays and customs issues

7. **Example: SPM Component Sourcing Flow**
    1. Design finalization (CAD + BOM)
    2. Classify parts (standard, bought-out, custom)
    3. Source suppliers for each category
    4. Send RFQs (Request for Quotations)
    5. Approve drawings/specs with vendors
    6. Place orders & track deliveries
    7. Inspect items on receipt
    8. Assemble & test in-house

Pro Tip: Vendor Development

- Build a trusted network of:
    - CNC machining shops
    - Fabricators
    - Automation parts dealers
- Keep multiple vendors for critical components to avoid bottlenecks.

Quality Checks & Tolerances in SPM Manufacturing

1. Why They Matter

In precision engineering and SPMs, even small deviations can:

- Lead to part mismatch or failure
- Affect machine performance and repeatability
- Increase wear and rework cost

Goal: Ensure every part fits, functions, and performs **as intended**, consistently.

2. What Are Tolerances?

Tolerance is the **permissible variation** in a dimension, ensuring part interchangeability and functionality.

Term	Meaning
Nominal size	Ideal dimension specified in the drawing
Tolerance	Acceptable upper and lower limit variation
Fit	Relationship between mating parts (e.g., shaft and hole)

Types of Fit

- **Clearance Fit**: Always leaves space (e.g., rotating shaft in bearing)
- **Interference Fit**: Parts press-fit tightly (e.g., gear mounted on a shaft)
- **Transition Fit**: May be snug or slightly loose depending on tolerance range

3. Common Tolerancing Standards

Standard	Use Area
ISO system	Global manufacturing practices
ANSI/ASME	Common in North America
IS codes	Indian manufacturing standards
GD&T	Geometric Dimensioning & Tolerancing (form, position, orientation)

GD&T is essential for controlling not just size but also **form, flatness, perpendicularity, concentricity**, etc.

4. Types of Quality Checks

Check Type	Purpose	Tools Used
Dimensional	Verify physical dimensions vs. drawing	Vernier caliper, micrometer, height gauge
Geometric	Check straightness, flatness, runout	Dial indicator, CMM, surface plate
Surface finish	Ensure smoothness or roughness limits	Surface roughness tester (Ra meter)
Visual inspection	Look for dents, cracks, poor welds, etc.	Naked eye, magnifier, borescope
Functional tests	Confirm assembly or operation	Trial runs, cycle tests, load tests
Material checks	Validate hardness or composition	Hardness tester, spectrometer, UTM

5. **Quality Checkpoints in SPM Manufacturing**
    1. **Raw Material Inspection**
        - Verify grade, size, and supplier certification
    2. **In-Process Inspection**
        - First-piece approval, sample checks during machining/ fabrication
    3. **Final Dimensional Inspection**
        - 100% or sampling, based on tolerance sensitivity
    4. **Assembly Checks**
        - Alignment, smooth movement, correct fits
    5. **Pre-dispatch Inspection**
        - Functional testing, vibration test, trial runs
6. **Tolerance Example**

Part	Nominal Size	Tolerance	Allowable Range
Shaft	Ø20.00 mm	±0.02 mm	19.98 – 20.02 mm
Mounting hole	Ø20.10 mm	+0.05/-0.00 mm	20.10 – 20.15 mm
Flatness of surface	N/A	0.02 mm max	Surface variation ≤0.02 mm

7. **Best Practices for Quality Assurance**

- Use a **calibrated tool** set and maintain up-to-date calibration records.
- Follow structured **inspection plans** tied to critical tolerances.
- Apply **3rd-party QC** or **CMM reports** for customer-specified tolerances.
- Store parts in clean, labeled, protected conditions post-inspection.

Wiring, Tubing, and Assembly Procedures

Efficient wiring, neat tubing, and systematic assembly are crucial in ensuring the **safety, functionality, and maintainability** of Special Purpose Machines (SPMs).

1. **Electrical Wiring**

   Purpose: Connects sensors, actuators, HMIs, motors, and control systems (like PLCs) in a safe and organized manner.

Best Practices

- Use **color-coded wires** for easy identification (e.g., red for +24V, black for 0V).
- Route wires through **conduits or cable trays** to avoid tangling or damage.
- Keep **separate routing for power and signal lines** to reduce noise/interference.
- Use **numbered ferrules and wire tags** for troubleshooting ease.
- Ensure **proper earthing/grounding** of all electrical components.
- Provide **terminal blocks and junction boxes** with clear labels.

Materials Used

- PVC/FRLS wires
- Cable drag chains (for moving parts)
- DIN rail terminals, relays, connectors

2. **Pneumatic and Hydraulic Tubing**

   Purpose: Carries compressed air (pneumatics) or oil (hydraulics) to actuators like cylinders and valves.

Best Practices:

- Use **PU tubes or flexible hoses** with appropriate pressure ratings.
- Follow **color coding** (e.g., blue for air, red for oil).
- Keep bends smooth and avoid sharp turns to reduce pressure loss.
- Install **flow restrictors** or mufflers where needed for speed and noise control.
- Use **push-to-connect fittings** for easy maintenance.
- Prevent leakage by using **Teflon tape** or thread sealant at joints.

Safety Tip: Always depressurize the system before performing any maintenance.

3. **Mechanical Assembly Procedures**

Objective: To ensure all components are assembled as per drawing and function seamlessly.

Assembly Steps:

1. **Base Setup:**
   - Level the machine frame using precision spirit levels or digital inclinometers.
2. **Component Mounting:**
   - Install motors, slides, gearboxes, sensors, etc., in sequence.
   - Use torque wrenches to ensure correct tightening.

3. **Fixture and Tooling Assembly**

- Install clamps, guides, jigs, and tool holders.
- Check for correct alignment and motion.

4. **Wiring and Tubing Integration**
   - Route cables and tubes only after mechanical mounting to avoid interference.
5. **Final Checks**
   - Run dry cycles to ensure smooth operation.
   - Check for noises, binding, or overheating.
6. **Documentation and Testing**

   Maintain:
   - Assembly checklist (component-by-component)
   - Wiring diagrams and pneumatic circuit drawings
   - Part serial numbers and calibration data
   - Trial run reports and test logs

   Final validation includes:
   - Functional test
   - Vibration or noise check
   - Safety interlock test
   - Visual and dimensional inspection

In Summary

Aspect	Key Focus
Wiring	Neat layout, safe routing, color codes, grounding
Tubing	Pressure rating, leak prevention, clean installation
Assembly	Stepwise process, torque control, alignment
Testing	Verify all functions before delivery

CHAPTER 7

Testing and Commissioning

"Machines follow logic.
Success follows clarity."

Dry Run & Functional Testing in SPMs

1. What Is a Dry Run?

A **dry run** is a **preliminary, no-load test cycle** of a machine or process, performed **without actual workpieces or materials**. It verifies that mechanical and control systems work correctly before real production begins.

Purpose:

- Validate mechanical motions, timing, and sequences
- Check alignment, safety interlocks, and actuator response
- Ensure program logic (PLC) is correct before production

When to Perform:

- After machine assembly
- Post-maintenance or upgrades
- Before first-time production

What to Check in a Dry Run:

Element	Check For
Mechanical motion	Smoothness, alignment, end positions
Sensors/limit switches	Proper triggering, no false signals
Air/oil supply systems	No leaks, correct pressures
Actuators & cylinders	Full stroke, no jerky motion
Tool paths (if CNC)	No collision, correct direction
PLC logic	Sequence of events is correct
HMIs and alarms	Proper display and diagnostics

Tip: Start at low speed to ensure safe observation.

2. **What Is Functional Testing?**

Functional testing simulates real production conditions using actual parts or materials. It validates machine performance, reliability, and output quality.

Purpose:

- Validate real-time operation with actual components or workpieces
- Confirm cycle time, accuracy, force, and tool engagement
- Ensure safety features operate under working conditions

When to Perform:

- After successful dry run
- Before machine handover or customer FAT (Factory Acceptance Test)
- During commissioning or troubleshooting

What to Check in Functional Testing:

Function	Test For
Workpiece handling	Correct clamping, alignment, ejection
Tool operation	Accuracy, force, depth, wear rate
Cycle time	Within acceptable limits
Product output	Meets quality specs, tolerances
Safety systems	Emergency stop, interlocks, guards
Feedback loops	Sensors triggering correct responses
Communication	PLC-HMI, SCADA integration working

Tip: Perform multiple test cycles to confirm **consistency and stability**.

3. Dry Run vs. Functional Test: At a Glance

Aspect	Dry Run	Functional Test
Load	No part/tool engagement	With actual parts and tools
Focus	Motion, logic, timing	Output quality, accuracy, reliability
Timing critical?	Not always	Yes, cycle time and efficiency measured
Safety tested?	Interlocks, yes	Full safety system under real conditions
Result	Mechanical readiness	Operational readiness

4. **Best Practices**
   - Document test results using structured **checklists** and **commissioning reports**.
   - Involve **mechanical, electrical, and automation teams** during testing.
   - Simulate edge cases (e.g., sensor failure, power cut).
   - Video-record final functional test as part of machine validation or FAT protocol.

   Would you like:
   - A **sample dry run checklist**
   - A **functional test report template**

A **FAT (Factory Acceptance Test) format** for your SPM commissioning or quality assurance documentation? If so, you can reach out to me via mail. I have dropped my mail ID at the last section of this book.

Calibration & Debugging in SPMs

1. **What is Calibration?**

   Calibration is the process of **adjusting instruments, sensors, and actuators** to ensure their outputs are **accurate and aligned with reference standards**.

   Purpose of Calibration in SPMs
   - Ensure precision in **positioning, force, pressure, temperature, and speed**
   - Maintain **tolerance limits**
   - Guarantee **repeatable and consistent results**

Key Components That Require Calibration

Component	Calibrated For	Tools Used
Linear actuators/slides	Travel distance, zero point	Dial gauge, laser measurement systems
Servo motors & encoders	Position feedback	HMI, tuning software, encoder tester
Pressure sensors	Setpoint accuracy	Master pressure gauge
Load cells	Force measurement	Calibration weights
Temperature sensors (RTDs)	Heat control	Thermocouple calibrator
Pneumatic regulators	Air pressure accuracy	Pressure gauge

Best practice: Use **traceable calibration standards** and recalibrate periodically (e.g., every 6–12 months).

2. **Calibration Process – General Steps**
   1. **Reference Check:** Compare component reading with a certified standard.
   2. **Adjustment:** If there's deviation, adjust hardware/ software values.
   3. **Verification:** Confirm that output now matches the desired target.
   4. **Documentation:** Record calibration date, method, values, and person responsible.

Example: Calibrating a Linear Slide

- Move the slide using servo to a supposed 200 mm position.
- Use a digital caliper or laser device to check actual position.
- If mismatch = 198.5 mm, adjust encoder scale factor or offset.
- Repeat for different points across the stroke and document.

3. **What is Debugging?**

Debugging is the process of **identifying and fixing issues or abnormal behaviors** in machine control logic, hardware wiring, or mechanical operations.

Common Areas Needing Debugging

System	Typical Issues
PLC programs	Incorrect logic, timer faults, scan delays
Sensors	False triggering, misalignment, loose wiring
Actuators	Jamming, wrong stroke, low force
HMIs	Wrong values displayed, communication loss
Motion systems	Position error, servo alarm, motor not starting

Debugging Process – Step by Step

1. **Replicate the Issue:** Try to consistently reproduce the error.
2. **Isolate the Problem:** Check mechanical, electrical, and program sections separately.

3. **Use Diagnostic Tools**
   - PLC online monitoring
   - Sensor/actuator signal simulators
   - Motor tuning software
   - Oscilloscopes/multimeters
4. **Fix and Re-Test:** Apply the solution and run multiple test cycles to ensure stability.
5. **Document:** Record the root cause and fix for future reference.

Example: Debugging a Sensor Fault

- **Problem**: Machine doesn't start the cycle.
- **Check 1**: Verify if the part-present sensor is triggered.
- **Check 2**: Check PLC diagnostic screen – is the input turning ON?
- **Check 3**: If not, inspect wiring, tighten connectors, or replace sensors.
- **Check 4**: Once fixed, verify in HMI and perform a dry run again.

4. **Best Practices for Calibration & Debugging**
   - Always **label all calibrated instruments** with date and next due date.
   - Maintain **calibration certificates** and logs.
   - Use **version control** for PLC and HMI programs.
   - Create a **debug logbook** for recurring machine issues.
   - Use **simulation mode** in PLCs when possible for safe debugging.

Safety Validation in SPMs

What Is Safety Validation?

Safety validation is the process of **verifying and confirming** that all safety features, controls, and systems of a machine **function correctly** and **meet defined safety standards** before use.

It ensures:

- Operator safety
- Compliance with regulations (CE, ISO, OSHA, etc.)
- Prevention of accidents and machine damage

1. **Key Areas to Validate**

Area	Validation Focus
Emergency stops (E-stops)	Must stop all motion immediately, from any point
Interlocks	Guards, doors must lock/disable motion when open
Two-hand controls	Both buttons must be pressed simultaneously for activation
Safety relays/ PLCs	All fail-safe logic must perform as programmed
Sensors & switches	Position, presence, and limit sensors must work reliably
Alarms & warnings	Audio/visual alerts must trigger for faults or hazards
Overload protection	Motors and actuators should not exceed safe load limits

Pressure/ temperature safety	Automatic shutdown on unsafe parameters

2. Safety Validation Checklist

Mechanical Safety

- Sharp edges removed or covered
- Moving parts guarded or enclosed
- Pinch/crush points eliminated or minimized
- All clamps and fixtures secured

Electrical Safety

- Emergency stops tested
- Earth grounding verified
- Overcurrent protection (fuses, breakers)
- Control panel labeled and locked

Control System Safety

- PLC safety logic tested (forced inputs/outputs)
- Redundancy where required (dual-channel safety relays)
- Safety inputs override normal operation
- Faults are logged and trigger shutdown

Operator Interface

- HMI displays clear warnings/errors
- Manual/auto switch works correctly
- Clear labels and pictograms on machine
- Operating manual available and accessible

3. Functional Safety Testing Methods

Test Type	Purpose
E-stop function test	Verifies immediate power-off and motion stop
Guard door test	Machine must not run if doors are open
Power loss simulation	Safe stop/restart behavior after power failure
Sensor bypass attempt	Confirms machine halts when safety sensors fail or are bypassed
Load/overtravel test	Checks behavior when machine exceeds limits

Tip: Record **"before vs after" test conditions** to confirm proper correction of safety issues.

4. Validation Standards to Follow

Standard	Scope
ISO 13849-1	Control system safety (Performance Level rating)
IEC 60204-1	Electrical safety in industrial machines
ISO 12100	General machine safety principles
OSHA/ANSI (USA)	Workplace and operator safety regulations
CE Marking (Europe)	Overall machine safety compliance

5. **Documentation & Reporting**

   A full **Safety Validation Report** should include:

   - Risk assessment summary
   - Safety circuit test results
   - Completed validation checklist (signed by QA/Safety Officer)
   - Calibration certificates (where applicable)
   - Operator training records
   - Safety control system diagrams

6. **Example: Safety Validation in Practice**

   Machine: Pneumatic press in an SPM

   Validated Items:

   - Two-hand control works → Only activates press if both buttons held
   - **Emergency stop:** Cuts off pneumatic & electrical supply
   - **Guard interlock:** Press disabled when guard is open
   - **Pressure regulator:** Limits force below 3.5 bar

   Result: All features passed → Signed off for production.

Summary: Why Safety Validation Matters

Benefit	Outcome
Prevents injuries	Ensures operator safety
Reduces downtime	Avoids machine damage from unsafe actions
Meets legal compliance	Prevents regulatory fines, bans, or shutdown
Builds customer trust	Safer, certified machines

CHAPTER 8

MAINTENANCE AND TROUBLESHOOTING

> *"Fixing is reactive. Maintaining is proactive. Improving is strategic."*

Types of Maintenance: Preventive, Predictive, Breakdown

1. **Preventive Maintenance (PM)**

   Definition: Scheduled, routine maintenance tasks performed **before a failure occurs**.

   Purpose:

   - Avoid unexpected breakdowns
   - Increase machine lifespan
   - Maintain consistent performance

   Examples:

   - Cleaning filters every 2 weeks
   - Lubricating moving parts monthly
   - Checking fasteners and belts quarterly
   - Replacing oil and seals annually

Frequency:

- Based on **time, usage hours, or production cycles**

Benefits:

Pros	Cons
Reduces unplanned downtime	May cause unnecessary part replacements
Increases reliability	Requires machine shutdowns for checks

2. **Predictive Maintenance (PdM)**

Definition: Maintenance based on ***real-time data*** from sensors and analytics, carried out **just before a failure is likely to occur**.

Techniques Used:

- Vibration analysis
- Thermography (infrared)
- Oil analysis
- Condition monitoring sensors (e.g., motor current, temperature)

Example:

- Replacing a bearing only when vibration exceeds threshold
- Adjusting pneumatic system pressure before seal wear causes leakage

Benefits:

Pros	Cons
Minimizes unplanned downtime	Requires advanced monitoring tools
Extends component life	Higher initial setup and training cost
Reduces maintenance cost over time	Data interpretation requires expertise

3. **Breakdown Maintenance (Reactive)**

   Definition: Maintenance performed **after equipment fails** or breaks down.

   Example:

   - Fixing a jammed actuator
   - Replacing a burnt-out motor
   - Repairing a snapped timing belt

Benefits:

Pros	Cons
No upfront maintenance cost	High downtime and potential production loss
Simple to plan	Risk of secondary damage or safety hazards

Comparison Table

Aspect	Preventive	Predictive	Breakdown
Based on	Time/Usage schedule	Real-time condition	After failure
Tools needed	Checklists, tools	Sensors, analytics	Basic tools
Cost (long-term)	Medium	Low (after setup)	High
Downtime risk	Low	Very low	Very high
Skill requirement	Low to moderate	High	Moderate

Best Practice in SPMs

Use a **combined maintenance strategy** for optimal results:

- **Preventive** for routine tasks (cleaning and lubrication)
- **Predictive** for critical components (spindles, drives, and valves)
- **Breakdown** only as a backup when unexpected failure occurs

Common Issues in SPMs

1. Mechanical Issues

Problem	Cause	Impact
Misalignment of moving parts	Improper assembly, worn bearings	Inaccurate operations, part rejection

Excessive vibration or noise	Unbalanced rotating parts, loose fasteners	Reduced precision, component fatigue
Clamping failure	Weak pneumatic/ hydraulic force, seal leakage	Unsafe operations, poor part holding
Premature wear of components	Lack of lubrication, wrong material selection	High maintenance, frequent downtime
Sticking or jerky motion	Dirty guide rails, damaged actuators	Slower cycle time, accuracy issues

2. Electrical & Automation Issues

Problem	Cause	Impact
Sensor malfunction	Wiring faults, misalignment, dirty environment	Sequence failure, false alarms
PLC logic errors	Programming bugs, missing interlocks	Unexpected machine stops
Cable wear or breakage	Repeated motion, improper routing	Power/signal loss, sporadic failures
Inconsistent actuator behavior	Voltage drops, faulty solenoids	Cycle variation, safety risks
Servo motor faults	Overload, encoder misreading	Positioning errors, motion failures

3. Pneumatic & Hydraulic Issues

Problem	Cause	Impact
Air/oil leakage	Worn seals, cracked fittings, loose connections	Pressure drop, clamping failure
Cylinder not extending/ retracting	Solenoid valve failure, air lock	Stuck motion, failed operation
Pressure not maintained	Regulator failure, blocked lines	Reduced force, safety compromise

4. Control & Software Issues

Problem	Cause	Impact
HMI not responding	Touchscreen damage, firmware crash	Operator unable to start or monitor cycle
SCADA/PLC communication failure	IP conflict, port blocking, faulty cables	Data loss, control delays
Alarm messages unclear or missing	Poor programming or incorrect language settings	Slows down troubleshooting

5. Operational & Human Errors

Problem	Cause	Impact
Wrong part loaded	Lack of part verification or sensors	Misprocessing, tool damage

Improper tool installation	Human error, no tool ID system	Cycle failure, safety hazard
Skipped maintenance	Poor scheduling or follow-up	Long-term reliability issues
Untrained operator	No SOP or training provided	Frequent stoppages, misuse of functions

6. **Inspection & Output Quality Issues**

Problem	Cause	Impact
Inconsistent part quality	Tool wear, calibration drift	High rejection rate, rework cost
Dimensional variations	Thermal expansion, tool offset error	Non-conformance with tolerances
Burrs, scratches, poor finish	Dull tools, incorrect feed rates	Customer dissatisfaction

Quick Troubleshooting Tips

- Always check **sensor indicators and PLC status** first
- Use **dry run mode** to isolate motion-related problems
- Keep a **fault logbook** to identify recurring issues
- Train operators to recognize early signs (noise, delays, overheating)
- Implement **preventive & predictive maintenance** schedules

Maintenance Scheduling for SPMs

Objective:

To **plan, prioritize, and execute** maintenance activities **before failures occur**, ensuring continuous, safe, and efficient operation of machines.

1. Types of Maintenance to Schedule

Type	Includes	Schedule
Daily Checks	Visual inspection, cleaning, air/oil pressure, emergency stops	Start of each shift
Weekly	Lubrication, sensor cleaning, basic actuator check	Once per week
Monthly	Belt/chain tension, electrical connections, filter cleaning	Every 30 days
Quarterly	Alignment check, calibration, detailed visual inspection	Every 3 months
Annual	Overhaul, safety audit, PLC/HMI backup, deep cleaning	Yearly (or shutdown)
Predictive	Based on vibration, temperature, run hours (using sensors/analytics)	As needed

2. What to Include in a Maintenance Schedule

Field	Description
Machine name/ID	Unique identifier for each SPM
Component or part	The specific part to be checked (e.g., guide rail, solenoid)
Task to perform	Action needed (e.g., clean, lubricate, tighten, calibrate)
Frequency	Daily, weekly, monthly, etc.
Assigned to (Technician)	Person/team responsible
Due date	When the task should be completed
Status	Pending, In-progress, Completed
Remarks/Findings	Notes on wear, faults, or replacements

3. Tools for Scheduling

- **Manual systems:** Excel sheets, whiteboards (suitable for small teams)
- **Software-based:**
  - CMMS (Computerized Maintenance Management Systems) like:
    - Fiix
    - UpKeep
    - Maintenance Connection
- ERP with a maintenance module (SAP, Odoo, TallyPrime+)

Tip: Use **QR codes or RFID tags** on machines to access mobile checklist access and track maintenance history in real-time.

4. **Integration with Production**
    - Schedule maintenance **during shift changes or low-production hours**
    - Maintain **buffer time** before major projects or customer FAT
    - Use **downtime dashboards** to track trends and plan better
5. **Example: Weekly Maintenance Schedule (Excerpt)**

Day	Machine	Task	Technician	Status	Remarks
Mon	SPM-Drill01	Lubricate spindle slide	Ajay	Done	No issues found
Tue	SPM-Weld02	Clean cooling fans	Reena	Pending	Dust buildup
Wed	SPM-Pack03	Check sensor alignment	Ravi	In-Progress	Slight offset

Best Practices

- Use **color-coded calendars** for visual clarity
- Track **machine run hours** to schedule maintenance by usage
- Maintain a **logbook or digital maintenance history**
- Set up **reminders/alerts** via email or app
- Always follow up with **post-maintenance verification**

Tools and Software Used in SPMs

1. Design & Engineering Software

Software	Purpose	Example Tools
CAD (2D/3D)	Mechanical part and assembly design	AutoCAD, SolidWorks, Siemens NX, CATIA
CAE/FEA	Stress analysis, motion simulation	ANSYS, Altair HyperWorks, Solid Edge
CAM	CNC toolpath generation	Mastercam, Fusion 360, Edgecam
Electrical CAD	Panel layout, wiring diagrams	EPLAN, AutoCAD Electrical, SEE Electrical
Fluid Simulation	Pneumatic/ Hydraulic circuit simulation	FluidSIM, Automation Studio

2. Automation & Control Software

System	Purpose	Popular Tools
PLC Programming	Machine logic control	Siemens TIA Portal, Allen Bradley RSLogix
HMI/SCADA Design	Operator interface, real-time monitoring	WinCC, FactoryTalk View, InduSoft, Ignition

Motion Control	Servo/stepper tuning and configuration	Delta ASDA Soft, Mitsubishi MR Configurator
Robot Programming	Teaching and simulation	ABB RobotStudio, KUKA WorkVisual

3. Production & Fabrication Tools

Tool Type	Purpose	Examples
Measuring instruments	Accuracy and tolerance verification	Vernier caliper, micrometer, height gauge
Assembly tools	Build and fit components	Torque wrenches, Allen keys, screwdrivers
CNC machines	Precision part fabrication	VMC, turning center, wire EDM
Welding & fabrication	Structure and bracket building	MIG, TIG welders, grinders
Sheet metal tools	Panel and enclosure work	Laser cutter, press brake, shear cutter

4. Diagnostic & Maintenance Tools

Tool	Purpose	Used For
Multimeter	Electrical checks	Voltage, continuity, current
Vibration analyzer	Predictive maintenance	Bearing health, imbalance

Thermal camera	Hotspot detection	Motors, panels, wiring
Air leak detector	Pneumatics troubleshooting	Leak diagnosis in tubing and fittings
CMM (Coordinate Machine)	3D precision measurement	Geometric accuracy of machined parts

5. Project Management & Documentation

Tool	Purpose	Examples
Project tracking	Timeline, resource, BOM tracking	Microsoft Project, Trello, Monday.com
Version control	Software versioning	Git, SVN, Siemens Teamcenter
Documentation	Manuals, SOPs, wiring logs	MS Word/Excel, Notion, Google Workspace

6. Optional Smart Tech for Industry 4.0 (Advanced SPMs)

Tech	Purpose	Example Tools/ Platforms
IIoT Platforms	Real-time data capture and analytics	ThingWorx, MindSphere, Azure IoT
Digital Twin	Simulation of real machine in software	Siemens NX, Dassault 3DEXPERIENCE

Remote diagnostics	Remote monitoring and debugging	TeamViewer, MQTT-based dashboards
Cloud CMMS	Maintenance scheduling and asset tracking	UpKeep, Fiix, IBM Maximo

Summary Table

Area	Primary Tools/Software
Design & Simulation	SolidWorks, AutoCAD, ANSYS, FluidSIM
Automation & Control	Siemens TIA Portal, RSLogix, WinCC, FactoryTalk
Fabrication & Assembly	CNC machines, hand tools, welding equipment
Measurement & Testing	CMM, dial indicators, multimeters, thermal cameras
Maintenance & Monitoring	Vibration sensors, CMMS, thermal imaging, leak detectors
Project Management	Excel, Notion, Teamcenter, Microsoft Project

CHAPTER 9

SUCCESS STORIES AND TESTIMONIALS

> *"Every great solution was once a rejected idea."*

Case Studies

- We've created solutions that reduced manpower from **750 to just 30.**
- We also developed a **Socket Assembly solution** that brought down the requirement from **32 operators to just 3**, while producing **30,000 units**.
- Over time, we have developed **more than 300 import-substitute machines**, offering functionality at **half the cost** of their foreign counterparts.

MCB Assembly Line

When the country's electrical infrastructure was being geared up with the mandatory sort of induction of **MCBs as a safety device**, we developed an **automated assembly line** to revolutionize the manufacturing process. It enabled functioning in **three shifts with just 4 operators** instead of 40.

Universal Joint Assembly (Japanese Company)

With no availability of technology that could completely automate the process of **Universal Joint assembly** for consistent production, we took up the challenge for a **Japanese company** and evolved a machine for flawless assembly, without the intervention of an operator.

We repeated the feat with another landmark development in the country: a **Balancing Machine** for the precise and calibrated locking mechanism of the power-steering column, matching the performance of Japanese machines.

Cluster Switch Assembly

Holding high esteem for the country in European competition, we successfully designed a fully automated setup for **Viney/ Vimercati**, comprising **44 multimode operative stations** to function with just **2 operators instead of 30** for assembling a **Cluster-Switch** of a hi-end European passenger vehicle. The line also featured an **auto-calibrated multi-model changeover**.

Single Phase & Three Phase Energy Meters

The landmark administrative decision of the government to replace the energy metering devices pan India only with **domestically manufactured Smart Energy Meters** called for a multi-fold scaling up of test-facilities, as each meter undergoes multi-function verifications in serial order. We designed a parallel flow system that **tested and rolled out each device within 30 seconds** as compared to the traditional **5 to10 minute cycle**.

FMCG Automation – Consumer Products

Addressing the automation demands of commercial fast-moving consumer goods has always been an engineering challenge anywhere in the world. We conceptualized and developed a **fully-automated and integrated assembly cum functional-test line** for **a Consumer Products** division to produce **25000 units per day** of the high-turnover mosquito repellent flash device by making use of only two operators as against sixty in the **existing manual-mechanized set-up.**

Technology Patent–

A technology patent is under approval for critical-care Medical Bed that has been uniquely designed for the comfort of patients during and after the surgical activities.

CHAPTER 10

FUTURE OF SPMs

"In the world of machines, precision is compassion."

Modular Design Trends in SPMs

What is Modular Design?

Modular design is an approach where a machine is built from **standardized, interchangeable units or modules**. Each module performs a specific function and can be upgraded, replaced, or reconfigured independently.

1. **Key Trends in Modular SPM Design**

   A. **Plug-and-Play Modules**

   - Pre-assembled units (e.g., feeder, press, inspection station) that can be added or removed without extensive rewiring.
   - Quick commissioning → faster project turnarounds

   B. **Standardized Interfaces**

   - Mechanical, electrical, and software interfaces follow uniform standards (e.g., IO-Link, M12 connectors).
   - Reduces integration time and complexity

C. Scalable Platforms

- Machines designed to grow with production needs.
    - **Example:** Start with 2 stations → scale to 5 as demand increases.
- Ideal for SMEs and contract manufacturers

D. Reconfigurable Tooling

- Tool modules can be swapped for new product versions without redesigning the whole machine.
- Speeds up product changeovers and reduces downtime

E. Software Modularization

- PLC programs built with modular blocks for motion, safety, vision, etc.
- Easier to debug, replicate, and update

2. Benefits of Modular Design in SPMs

Benefit	Impact
Faster development	Reduces design and build time
Simplified maintenance	Faulty modules can be replaced quickly
Cost-effective upgrades	Only specific modules need upgrading
Shorter downtime	Quick troubleshooting and repair
Flexibility in customization	Modules can be tailored for different clients

3. Common Modular Components in SPMs

Module	Function
Base frame modules	Adjustable frames with leveling feet
Pick & place units	Modular grippers/arms with servo/ pneumatics
Conveyor segments	Plug-in belt/roller sections
Inspection stations	Integrated camera + lighting blocks
Clamping modules	Standard pneumatic/electric clamps
HMI/operator panels	Detachable and configurable consoles

4. Industry Trends Driving Modularization

Trend	How Modular Design Helps
Industry 4.0 & Smart Factories	Easier integration of sensors and analytics modules
High-mix, low-volume production	Fast reconfiguration for different SKUs
Global machine supply	Module reuse across geographies, standard compliance
Rapid prototyping	Reuse mechanical and software building blocks

5. Real-world Example

Application: Modular Assembly Line for Automotive Switches
Modules:

- Base chassis with universal mounting slots
- Screwdriving module (XYZ servo)
- Vision inspection block (modular camera mount)

- Labeling unit
- Reject bin on slide-in drawer

When the client upgrades the switch model → only the inspection module is replaced and the PLC block logic is updated.

6. **Design Considerations for Modular Machines**
   - Use **standard hole patterns and mounting grids**
   - Ensure **electrical connectors** are plug-safe and coded
   - Adopt **universal PLC templates** for motion and IO blocks
   - Provide **clear interface documentation** for each module

AI & Machine Learning in Predictive Performance for SPMs

Objective:

To use **AI and ML algorithms** to **predict, prevent, and optimize** machine performance before issues arise—minimizing downtime and maximizing productivity.

What Is Predictive Performance?

Predictive performance involves forecasting how a machine or process will behave in the future based on **historical and real-time data**.

With AI/ML:

- Machines **learn from past patterns** (vibrations, temperatures, part failures)
- They **predict faults**, suggest **maintenance windows**, or auto-optimize processes

1. **Key AI/ML Applications in SPMs**

Application	What It Does
Predictive Maintenance	Predicts component wear/failure based on sensor data (vibration, load, temp)
Anomaly Detection	Detects abnormal machine behavior in real time before failure occurs
Cycle Time Optimization	Learns from operations to suggest faster, more stable settings
Tool Life Prediction	Uses wear patterns to forecast tool replacement needs
Energy Efficiency Monitoring	Flags inefficient usage or machine idling
Production Quality Prediction	Predicts defect probability based on process parameters

2. **What Data Is Used?**

AI and ML systems rely on **time-series data** from various sources:

Source	Examples
Sensors	Vibration, temperature, pressure, RPM
Control systems	PLC logs, servo feedback, alarm history
Cameras	Vision data for surface/assembly defects
Operator inputs	HMI usage, part rejection notes
Environmental data	Ambient temperature, humidity

3. **Workflow: How It Works**
    1. **Data Collection:** From sensors, PLCs, SCADA, cameras
    2. **Preprocessing**: Cleansing, filtering, normalizing signals
    3. **Model Training:** Use historical data to train AI/ML models to recognize patterns
    4. **Real-time Inference:** Apply trained models on live machine data to make predictions
    5. **Actionable Output**: Alerts, dashboards, maintenance scheduling, or automatic shutdown
4. **Common Tools & Platforms Used**

Type	Popular Tools
IIoT Platforms	Siemens MindSphere, PTC ThingWorx, Azure IoT
AI/ML Frameworks	Python (scikit-learn, TensorFlow, PyTorch)
CMMS + AI Modules	IBM Maximo, Fiix + ML plugins
Edge AI Devices	Nvidia Jetson, Siemens Industrial Edge, Rockwell AI

5. Benefits of AI in Predictive Performance

Benefit	Result
Early warning of failures	Reduced downtime, safer operations
Smarter maintenance	Replace parts only when needed
Process optimization	Higher throughput, better consistency

Quality improvement	Reduced rejects, proactive tuning
Cost savings	Fewer emergency repairs, optimal resource utilization

Example: AI in an SPM

Machine: High-speed rotary assembly machine

Problem: Intermittent jam and early tool wear

Solution:

- AI model trained on sensor + motor load data
- Detected micro-load spikes 2 hours before failure
- Alerted maintenance team → tool replaced pre-emptively

Result: 85% reduction in unexpected stoppages

6. Challenges and Considerations

Challenge	Solution
Need for large datasets	Start with high-priority assets
Noise in industrial data	Use robust filtering and AI preprocessing
Lack of skilled manpower	Use plug-and-play platforms (low-code AI)
Integration with legacy systems	Adopt edge devices or gateway modules

BONUS CHAPTER: INSIGHTS, CHALLENGES & SUSTAINABILITY

> *"Experience builds machines.*
> *Reflection builds mastery."*

Why Automation Fails

Real-world hurdles and blind spots that lead to failed automation—plus a joint mindset for turning failures into success.

- "One Size Fits All" mindset
- A hazy picture of the final objective and result expected from automation
- Inconsistent dimensional tolerance w.r.t. drawing and the physically available child part(s)
- Wide dimensional differences in actual part vs. the dimensions mentioned in RFQ/DAP/trials
- Augmentations and changes in sequence/process during the phase of development/manufacture
- Vital decision on — When to use automation

- Understanding the difference between a "Standard Product" and a "Development Product"
- Replacing high-volume trials with low-volume trials to save time
- Insufficient parts availability during operational/functional validation

Theme — We jointly CAN iron out the bottlenecks for success and a win-win result.

3 Big Mistakes by Business Owners

- Quality of child part not designed for automation
- Not investing in machinery and relying on manual methods
- Not selecting proper equipment/machinery

Why Delivery Gets Delayed

- Requirement change after quotation
- Additional requirement after negotiation
- Design data not available
- Delay in design approval
- Child part not available during machine development & trial
- Child part quality not as per design data
- Machine BOP not available at supplier end

Our Focus Should be on Carbon Neutrality:

Carbon Neutrality is the concept of balancing the amount of carbon dioxide (CO_2) emitted into the atmosphere with an equivalent amount removed or offset, resulting in net-zero carbon emissions.

What Does It Mean?

When an individual, company, city, or country becomes carbon neutral, it means they:

1. Reduce carbon emissions as much as possible (e.g., using renewable energy, improving efficiency).
2. Offset the remaining emissions (e.g., by planting trees, investing in carbon capture projects, or buying carbon credits).

Why Is It Important?

Carbon dioxide is a major greenhouse gas, contributing to global warming and climate change. Reaching carbon neutrality is essential to:

- Limit the rise in global temperatures.
- Meet international goals like the Paris Agreement (which aims to limit warming to 1.5°C).
- Protect ecosystems, coastal cities, and future generations.

Who Is Aiming for Carbon Neutrality?

Many entities are making carbon-neutral pledges:

- **Countries:** e.g., India (by 2070), UK (by 2050), China (by 2060)
- **Companies:** Google (carbon neutral since 2007), Microsoft, Apple
- **Events:** The Olympics, large conferences, etc.

How Can You Help?

- Use energy-efficient appliances
- Reduce car/air travel or use electric vehicles

- Support renewable energy sources
- Consume less meat and more local produce
- Offset your personal carbon footprint online
- Use electrical actuators instead of pneumatic actuators
- Optimise pressure to adjust required force
- Use pressure regulator on return line where less pressure is sufficient

Air Leakage from Pipeline or Machine: A Hidden Energy Drain

1. **Fix Leaks**
   - **Up to 30%** of compressed air is lost through leaks.
   - Use **ultrasonic leak detectors** regularly.
   - Repair or replace faulty hoses, connectors, and seals promptly.
   - Implement a **leak detection and tagging program** with scheduled inspections.
2. **Use Efficient Pneumatic Components**
   - Replace outdated components with **low-consumption cylinders, valves, and actuators**.
   - Use **right-sized cylinders** (oversized ones waste air).
   - Install **flow restrictors** or **quick exhaust valves** to reduce consumption and cycle time.
3. **Optimize System Design**
   - Use **zoned compressed air** systems instead of one large system.
   - Isolate unused sections with **automated shut-off valves**.

- Design with **shorter, direct air lines** to reduce pressure drops.
- Employ **pressure boosters** only where necessary, not across the whole system.

4. **Regulate Air Pressure**
   - Don't set pressure higher than required—**every 1 bar increase = ~7% more energy usage**.
   - Use **pressure regulators** close to the point of use.
   - Install **pressure sensors** and monitor with **IoT dashboards** for real-time adjustments.
5. **Turn Off Air When Not in Use**
   - Use **automated shut-off valves** during machine idle or break periods.
   - Schedule air supply shut-off during nights and weekends.
   - Program PLCs to close air circuits when not needed.
6. **Recover and Reuse Exhaust Air**
   - Use **air-saving circuits** like air recovery systems to redirect exhaust air into other processes.
   - Install **blow-off air recovery systems** for non-contact air applications.
7. **Use Alternative Technologies**
   - Replace constant air blowers with **pulsed air** or **vacuum ejectors with air-saving features**.
   - Use **electromechanical actuators** instead of pneumatics for non-essential compressed air applications.
8. **Monitor & Benchmark**
   - Install **flow meters** to track air consumption per machine.
   - Conduct **energy audits** regularly.

- Benchmark performance and share data with teams to drive awareness and accountability.

9. **Employee Training**
   - Train operators and maintenance staff on **air-saving practices**.
   - Encourage **reporting of leaks or inefficiencies**.
   - Integrate air-saving tips into daily routines and SOPs.

Sustainability and Efficiency

- Reduce energy consumption by using **efficient motors** and **LED lighting**.
- Recycle waste materials and use **eco-friendly lubricants and coolants**.
- Implement **life cycle assessment** (LCA) for machines to reduce environmental impact.

Standard Operating Procedures (SOPs)

- Develop and follow **detailed SOPs** for each process to ensure consistency.
- Keep documentation updated with any changes in equipment or processes.

Supply Chain Integration

- Work closely with suppliers for **quality parts** and **on-time delivery**.
- Use **ERP systems** to manage inventory, production schedules, and procurement.

Closing Thought

> *"Perfection is a myth. Version one is better than version none."*

Thank you for giving your valuable time to read this book.

You've got almost like a Wikipedia of how to approach, plan, and succeed with **Special Purpose Machines (SPMs)**—from design and automation to maintenance, software, sustainability, and real-world challenges.

Now, you have two choices:

1. Use this book as your guide—your map—and move forward on your own.

OR

2. If you'd like me to walk alongside you, help decode a specific challenge, answer any query from the book, or explore how you can join hands with us—I'm here.

You can schedule a **1-to-1 meeting** with me directly at:

Email-ID: Kky@autotechindia.com

Scan this QR Code for contanct details

Let’s turn knowledge into action, together.

I’m committed to delivering the best service, cutting-edge automation, and reliable ROI to every client.

– Krishan Kumar

Awards That Inspire Us

Recognitions received over the years for innovation, service, and excellence.

TOYOTA BOSHOKU DEVICE INDIA
Best Performance of
QC Circle
Appreciation Awards
5th Vendor Group
Quality Circle Competition
November – 2024
Best Performance of QC Circle
Appreciation Award
4th Vendor
Group Quality Circle Competition
November – 2023
Shiroki Automotive India Pvt.Ltd
Bawal

A Glimpse of Innovation: Machines We're Proud Of

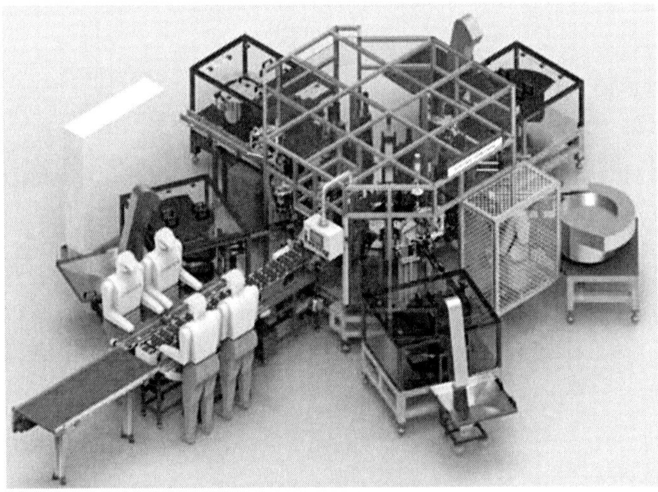

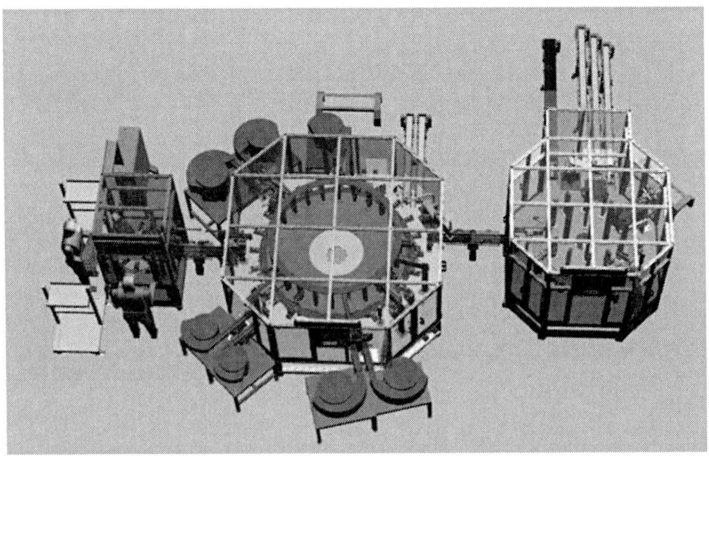

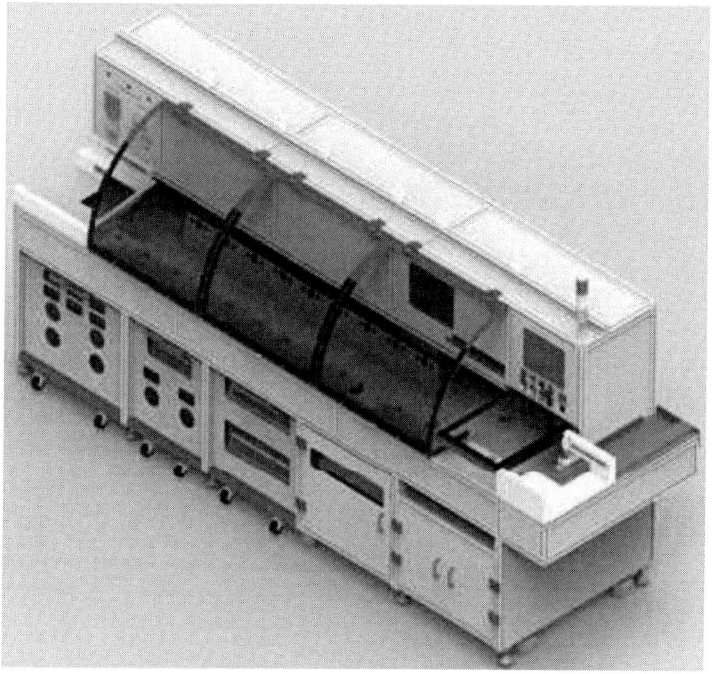

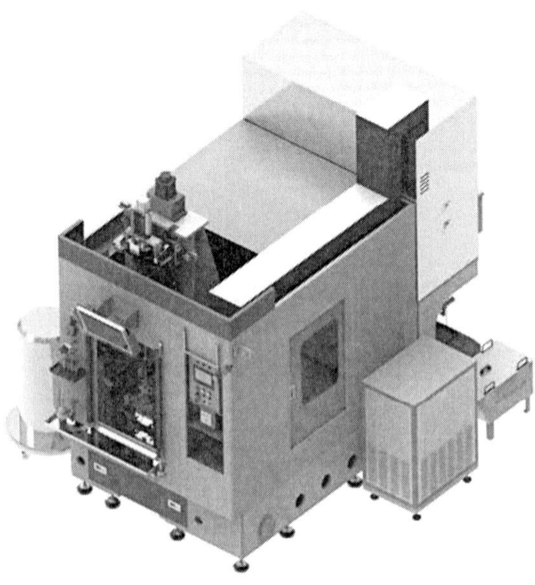